Christian Crafts from Cardboard

by Anita Reith Stohs

illustrated by Janet Skiles

Cover by Janet Skiles

Copyright © 1994

Shining Star Publications

ISBN No. 0-86653-779-1

Standardized Subject Code TA ac

Printing No. 98765432

Shining Star Publications
1204 Buchanan St., Box 299
Carthage, IL 62321-0299

Unless otherwise indicated, the New International Version of the Bible was used in preparing the activities of this book.

Dedication

To Thomas Paul: May your Lord and your God be with you as you grow in inches and in faith.

SS3812

Table of Contents

To the Teacher/Parent..................4

Old Testament

In the Beginning: Bookmark.................5

See What God Made: Nature Collage.......6

Thank God for Elephants: Stand-Up
Animal................7

God Made Me Special: Outline
Collage.................9

Safe from the Flood:
Ark and Animals.................10

A Rainbow of Promise:
Poster Collage.................13

Abraham and Sarah: Masks.................15

Daniel and the Lions:
Stick Puppets.................18

A Coat for Samuel:
Sewing Card.................19

The Lord Is My Shepherd:
Stand-Up Sheep.................21

Our Refuge and Strength: Castle.........23

New Testament

Get Ready for Jesus:
Advent Wreath.................25

Celebrate His Birth:
Cup Centerpiece.................27

Christ the Savior Is Born:
Nativity Scene.................29

We Have Seen His Star:
Tree Ornament.................35

A Dove Came Down: Mobile.............37

We Follow Jesus: Classroom
Mobile.................40

Through the Roof: Storytelling
House.................41

Jesus Loves Me: Silhouette Mobile....43

God's Love Is Forever: Shadow
Puppets.................45

Jesus Helps People: Stick Puppets......47

Sing Hosanna: Palm Sunday
Palm Branch.................51

He Is Risen: Pressed-Leaf Collage......53

The Holy Spirit Comes: Rice
Plaque.................55

Witness for the Lord: Aluminum
Foil Plaque.................57

Spread the Good Word: Boat.............59

Believe in Jesus: Cross Plaque.........62

Jumping for Joy: String Puppet.........63

To the Teacher/Parent

Children learn by doing. Crafts can provide children a chance to review Bible stories and their messages, both during the process of making the projects and later in the classroom or home. Such crafts, also, can serve as a witness to God's love in homes where parents are not involved in church. Use these crafts to actively involve your children in the Bible stories they have heard. As you make the projects, may you and the children come to a stronger faith in God, the maker of all things.

While pattern pieces are provided for those who want them, encourage children to draw for themselves as much as possible at their own developmental level. Pictures of finished crafts are intended to be used as suggestions only, not standards for how the projects have to be done.

Allow children creative freedom in doing the crafts presented in this book. Other ideas at the end of each activity are designed to provide you and the children with additional options in the construction of the projects. Allow children freedom to use their own, unique, God-given gifts of creativity as they find their own, individual interpretations of these and any crafts you do in their classroom.

In the Beginning

Bookmark

Bible Story:
God creates the heavens and earth. Genesis 1:1

Materials:
White poster board
Scissors
Colored tissue paper
Water
Paintbrush
Markers
Hole punch
Yarn
Tape

Directions:
1. Cut poster board into 2 1/2" x 6" strip.
2. Tear small pieces of tissue paper about 1" x 1 1/2" in size, using colors appropriate for the part of creation you wish to represent (mountains, woods, lakes, oceans, the sky, etc.).
3. Brush water over bookmark. Add colored tissue paper and let dry.
4. Pull off tissue paper and use a marker to write "God made the _____" (add the part of creation you are presenting) on the bookmark.
5. Punch holes about 1/2" apart around the edges of the bookmark.
6. Cut a 36" piece of yarn. Tie one end through a hole in the bookmark and tape the other end. Lace around the sides of the bookmark.

Other Ideas:
1. Make bookmarks to illustrate other Bible passages.
2. Omit tissue paper, and draw picture of creation on the bookmark.
3. Omit lacing.
4. Before punching holes and lacing edges, cover bookmark with clear adhesive plastic for more permanency.

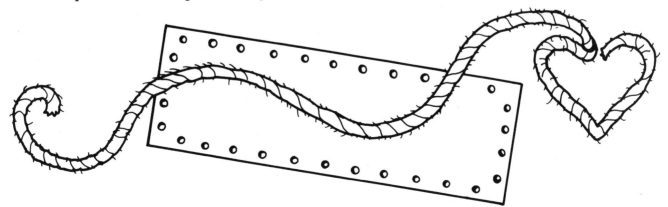

SS3812

See What God Made

Nature Collage

Bible Story:
God makes the earth and growing things. Genesis 1

Materials:
Cardboard
Blue tempera paint
Paintbrush
Tape
Nature objects
Glue
Scissors

Directions:
1. Cut a square of cardboard to desired size.
2. Paint square with tempera paint.
3. Go on a nature walk and gather small items suitable for gluing to cardboard.
4. Take the objects back to the classroom and glue them to the cardboard square.
5. Hang the collage to remind you to celebrate the many wonderful things God has put into our world.

Other Ideas:
1. Add this phrase to the bottom of the picture: "Thank God for His Wonderful World."
2. Glue nature objects to colored poster board.
3. Cover cardboard with burlap before adding objects.

SS3812

Thank God for Elephants

Stand-Up Animal

Bible Story:
God creates land animals. Genesis 1:24-25

Materials:
Poster board in assorted colors
Construction paper
Markers
Scissors
Pencil
Glue
Yarn

Directions:
1. Duplicate and cut out the patterns found on the following page. (Adult help may be needed.)
2. Trace the body shape on a piece of poster board and cut it out. Trace and cut out the ear shapes from construction paper.
3. Fold ears as indicated; then glue them to the elephant.
4. Cut a $3/4$" piece of yarn and glue it to the back of the elephant for a tail.
5. Write "Thank God for Elephants" on one side of the elephant.
6. Fold the elephant as indicated and stand it up. If needed, bend bottom of legs out slightly for better balance.
7. Elephants show God's mighty power of creation in many ways. Discuss some things elephants can do.

Other Ideas:
1. Make different kinds of stand-up animals.
2. Paint a piece of cardboard for the Garden of Eden, and make a variety of land animals to stand in front of it.
3. Cut animal shapes out of thin cardboard. Paint them and add details.
4. Omit construction paper ears. Draw them with markers instead.
5. Make up a thank-You prayer to God for the kind of animals you like best. Write the prayer on one side of your stand-up animal.
6. Read children's books about elephants to discover what a wonderful creation the elephant is and how man needs to take better care of it and other animals.

Elephant Patterns

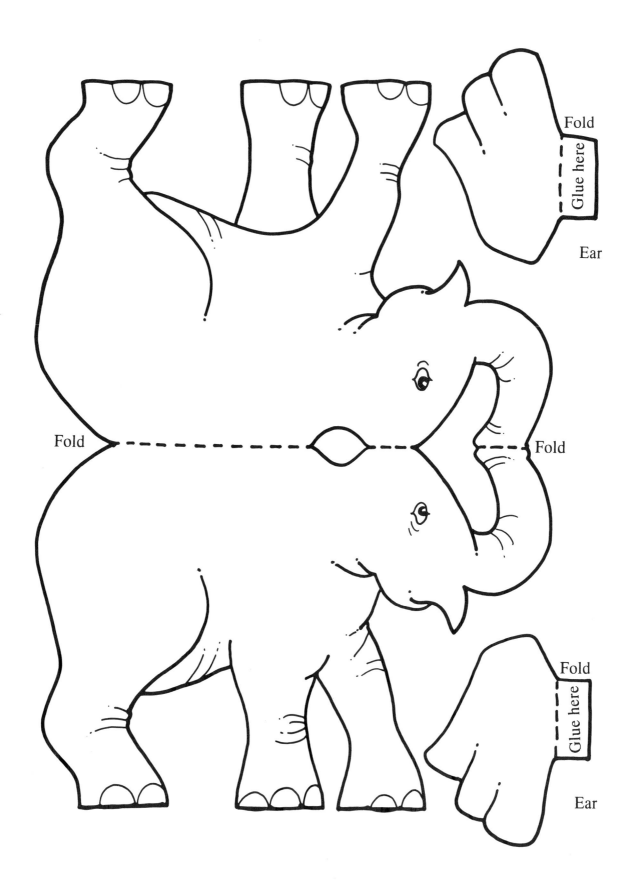

Fold

Glue here

Ear

Fold

Fold

Fold

Glue here

Ear

SS3812

God Made Me Special

Outline Collage

Bible Story:
God makes people. Genesis 1:27

Materials:
Cardboard
Construction paper
Scissors or knife (adults only)
Pencil
Glue
Markers

Directions:
1. Trace the outline of a body on a child-sized piece of cardboard.
2. Cut out the body shape.
3. Tear pieces of construction paper and glue them on for clothes, skin, hair, etc.
4. Use markers to draw on facial features and details.
5. Set the figures up against the wall, and thank God for making each one of us a special part of His creation.

Other Ideas:
1. Glue fabric scraps to the figures for clothes, or dress them in old clothes.
2. Cut a triangular cardboard brace and glue it to the back of the figure to make it stand up.
3. Paint the cardboard figure.
4. Draw a T-shirt on the figure saying, "God Made (Name) Special."
5. Outline figures and make them into Bible characters.

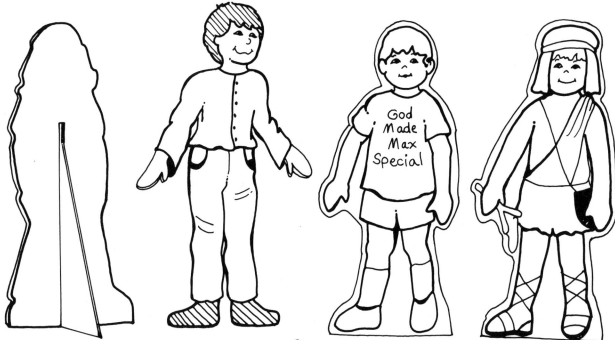

Shining Star Publications, Copyright © 1994
SS3812

Safe from the Flood

Ark and Animals

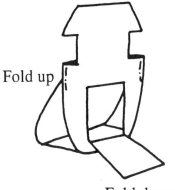

Bible Story:
The flood. Genesis 6-9

Materials:
Poster board
Scissors
Pencil
Fine-tipped markers
Stapler
Glue

Directions:

Ark

1. Duplicate and cut out the pattern found on page 11.
2. Trace and cut out ark pattern from poster board. Cut out ark door.
3. Fold ark as indicated below. Fold down door.
4. Staple ark hull together at sides.

Noah and the Animals

1. Duplicate animal and people patterns found on page 12.
2. Color animals and people with markers.
3. Cut out figures as indicated; then fold them so they will stand.
4. Use with the ark to tell the story of Noah and the Flood.

Other Ideas:

1. Make the ark from cardboard.
2. Paint the ark, people, and animals.
3. Cover ark with construction paper.
4. Let children draw their own pairs of animals to put in the ark.

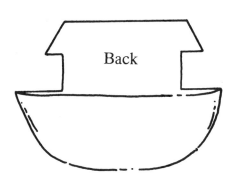

Back

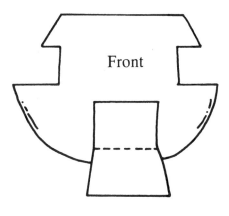

Front

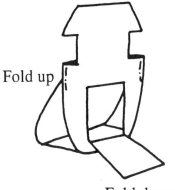

Fold up

Fold down

Ark Pattern

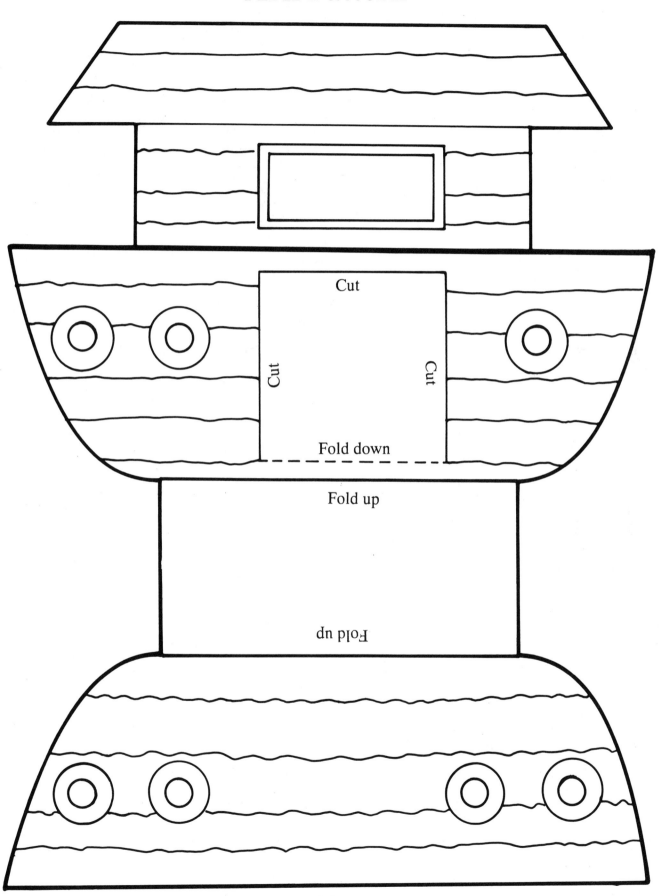

Ark

People and Animal Patterns

Noah   Mrs. Noah

Cut

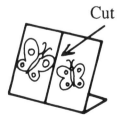

Cut out and fold up

SS3812

A Rainbow of Promise

Poster Collage

Bible Story:
God sets His rainbow in the sky. Genesis 9:8-17

Materials:
Blue poster board (9 ½" x 11")
Fabric scraps in rainbow colors
Cotton
Glue
Scissors

Directions:
1. Duplicate and cut out the pattern found on the following page.
2. Glue rainbow to poster board.
3. Cut square fabric pieces.
4. Glue fabric squares on poster board to make a rainbow.
5. Glue cotton to represent a cloud at bottom of rainbow.
6. Use a marker to write "God Keeps His Promises" on one side of the poster.
7. Let your rainbow be a reminder that we can rely on God to keep His promises to His people.

Other Ideas:
1. Paint a piece of cardboard blue.
2. Use squares of construction paper instead of fabric to color the rainbow.
3. Color rainbow with markers.
4. Use a prism to show how light breaks into different colors. Follow order of prism colors to color rainbow.
5. Use an overhead projector to enlarge rainbow pattern on larger piece of poster board.

Rainbow Pattern

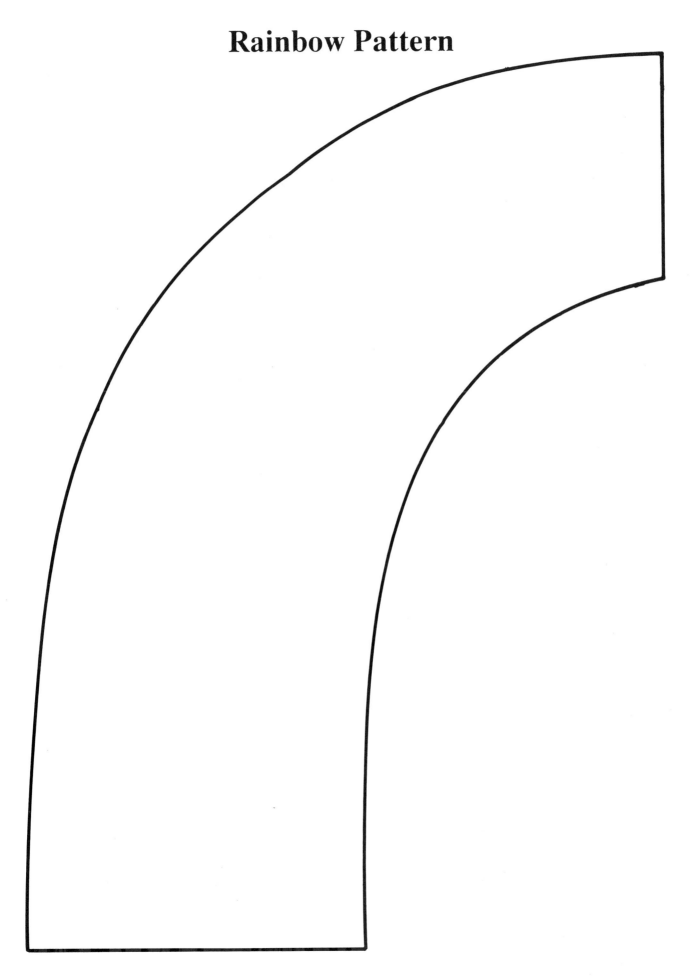

SS3812

Abraham and Sarah

Masks

Bible Story:
God promises a baby to Abraham and Sarah. Genesis 18:1-15

Materials:
Corrugated cardboard
Pink or light tan construction paper
Glue
Black yarn
Scissors

Directions:
1. Duplicate mask patterns found on pages 16-17. Cut out the outside and inside mask patterns, including eye and mouth holes.
2. Trace the outside of mask patterns A and C on cardboard and cut them out.
3. Trace the patterns for inside mask patterns B and D on construction paper and cut them out.
4. Glue mask pattern B on cardboard piece A. Glue mask pattern D on cardboard piece C.
5. Cut and glue yarn pieces on masks for hair and beard.
6. Cut eyes and mouths out of cardboard.
7. Cut holes on both sides of each mask where indicated. Cut and tie a 12" piece of yarn to each hole.
8. Wear masks and pretend to be Abraham and Sarah telling about how God promised them a son.

Other Ideas:
1. Drip paint or draw lines with a marker down ridges of corrugated cardboard.
2. Make masks out of solid pieces of cardboard.
3. Use mask shapes for other Bible stories.
4. Fit cardboard hair on a paper plate with eyes and mouth drawn on or cut out.
5. Draw eyes and mouths; then fasten cardboard masks to dowel sticks and use as puppets.

Abraham Pattern

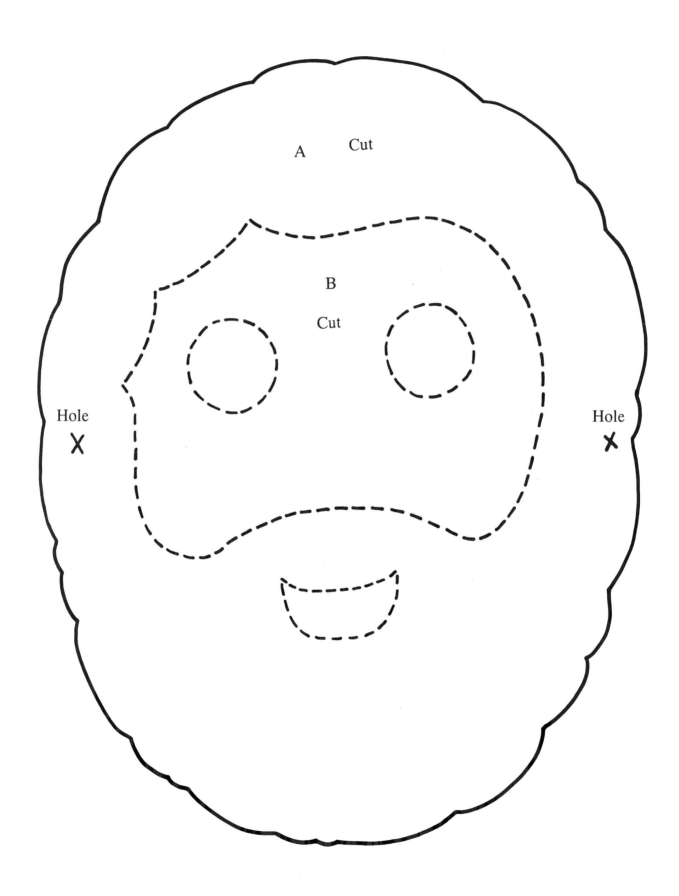

A   Cut

B

Cut

Hole   Hole

X   X

SS3812

Sarah Pattern

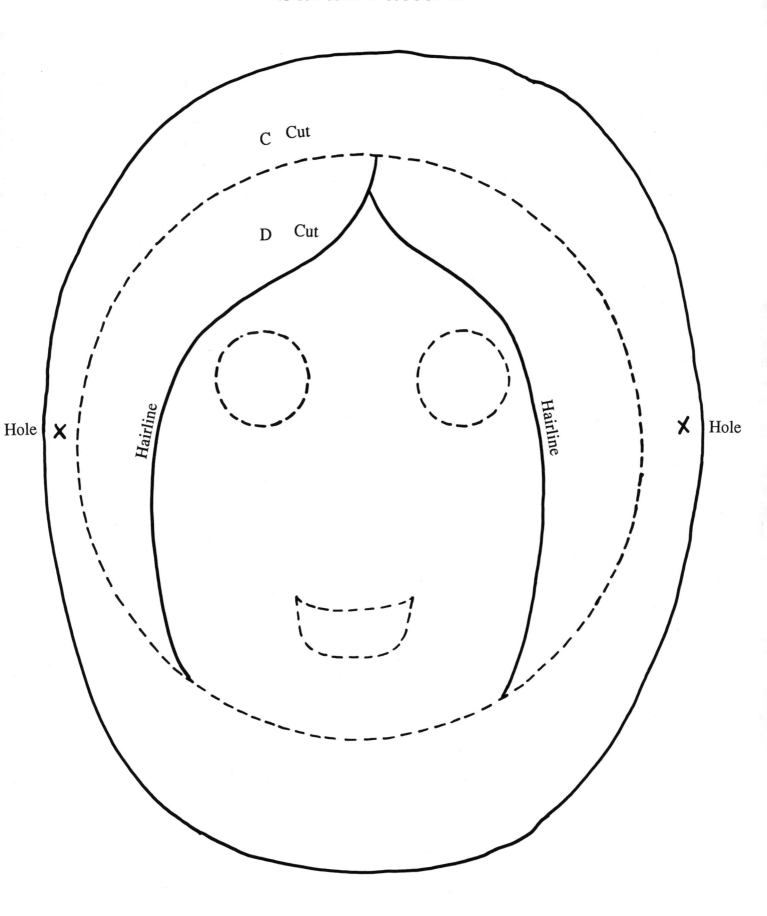

SS3812

Daniel and the Lions

Stick Puppets

Bible Story:
> Daniel in the lions' den. Daniel 6

Materials:
> Cardboard
> Construction paper (yellow and pink)
> Two craft sticks
> Glue
> Corrugated cardboard
> Markers
> Scissors

Directions:
1. Cut two construction paper circles (one of each color) and two cardboard circles the same size.
2. Glue construction paper circles to the cardboard circles.
3. Use markers to draw a lion's face on the yellow circle and Daniel's face on the pink circle.
4. Cut strips of corrugated cardboard.
5. Glue strips in a circle around the lion's face for a mane; then glue the strips onto Daniel's face for hair and a beard.
6. Tape each circle to a craft stick to make a puppet. Use the puppets to tell the story of how God protected Daniel in the den of hungry lions.

Other Ideas:
1. Glue corrugated cardboard strips around paper plates for masks.
2. Draw faces on circles cut from poster board.

A Coat for Samuel

Sewing Card

Bible Story:
Hannah visits Samuel in the temple. 1 Samuel 2:18-19

Materials:
Poster board
Marker
Hole punch
Fabric
Scissors
Glue
Yarn
Tape

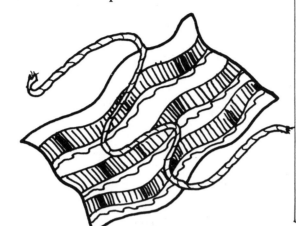

Directions:
1. Duplicate and cut out the robe pattern found on the following page.
2. Trace the robe pattern on a piece of fabric and cut it out.
3. Glue the fabric robe to the poster board.
4. Use the marker to write "A New Coat for Samuel" above the robe.
5. Punch holes, one inch apart, around the robe. For younger children, use fewer holes.
6. Cut a piece of yarn approximately 30" in length. Knot one end and tape the other end.
7. Pull the yarn through the holes as you pretend to be Hannah making a new coat for Samuel. Review the story of Hannah and Samuel in 1 Samuel 1:1-2:11, 18-21.
8. When finished, draw the feet, hands, and smiling face of Samuel, happy to have his new coat.

Other Ideas:
1. Outline the robe on the sewing card and glue fabric scraps on it.
2. Reuse the sewing card or tie a piece of yarn to the top and hang it as a picture.

Samuel's Coat Pattern

SS3812

The Lord Is My Shepherd

Stand-Up Sheep

Bible Story:
> The Lord is my Shepherd. Psalm 23

Materials:
> White poster board
> Scissors
> Glue
> Cotton
> Craft stick
> Styrofoam™ cup
> Fine-tip markers

Directions:
1. Duplicate and cut out the patterns found on the following page.
2. Trace and cut out a poster board sheep.
3. Use markers to outline the sheep's eye and mouth and to color the caption "The Lord Is My Shepherd."
4. Glue the craft stick and cotton to the sheep.
5. Trim the Styrofoam™ cup 2" from the bottom. Set it upside down and glue the caption on it.
6. Stick the bottom of the craft stick into the cup.
7. Let your stand-up sheep be a reminder that your loving Lord cares for you like a shepherd cares for his sheep.

Other Ideas:
1. Omit the cup and use the sheep alone for a puppet.
2. Make a cutout of Jesus, the Good Shepherd, to place beside the sheep.

"The Lord Is My Shepherd" Patterns

Our Refuge and Strength

Castle

Bible Story:
God–our helper. Psalm 46:1

Materials:
Cardboard
Glue
Scissors
Pencil
Construction paper
Felt-tip markers
Heavy-duty stapler

Directions:
1. Duplicate and cut out the patterns on the following page.
2. Cut an 18" x 11" rectangular piece of cardboard.
3. Use the rectangular pattern to trace and cut out rectangular openings across the top of the cardboard.
4. Trace and cut out arched windows from construction paper, using the window pattern. Glue the windows to the sides of the cardboard.
5. Cut out the doorway and use markers to decorate it. Glue it at the bottom of the cardboard.
6. Curve the cardboard into a circle. Staple it together with a 1" overlap.
7. Let this "castle" serve as a reminder that your strong God is always there to help and protect you.

Other Ideas:
1. Omit the pattern pieces and cut your own windows and door for the castle. Cut an arch for the door and write the Bible words on it.
2. Read the rest of Psalm 46, looking for other word pictures that tell of God's mighty power and protection in times of trouble.
3. Use with Bible lessons emphasizing God's protection in times of trouble.

Castle Patterns

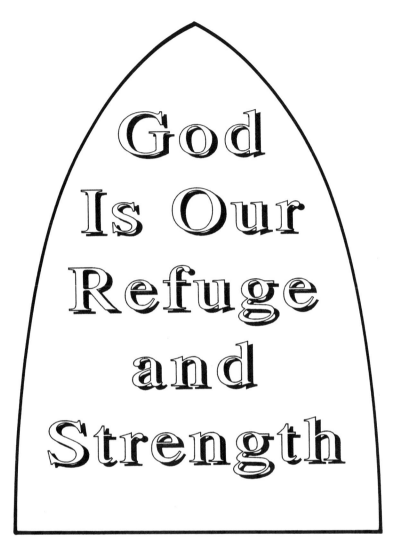

Doorway

Opening

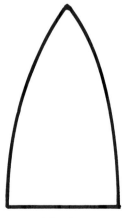

Window

Get Ready for Jesus

Advent Wreath

Bible Story:
God sends John to prepare people for the coming of Jesus. Luke 1:5-17

Materials:
Corrugated cardboard
Scissors
Green tempera paint
Paintbrush
Red tissue paper
Markers or crayons
Paper plate
Pencil
Yarn
Hole punch
Glue

Directions:
1. Duplicate and cut out patterns found on the following page.
2. Trace and cut out wreath pattern from corrugated cardboard. Paint green and let dry.
3. Color and cut out bow pattern.
4. Glue bow to wreath.
5. Punch a hole at the top of the wreath and tie a piece of yarn to it for hanging.
6. Cut twenty-five 1 ¹/₂" x 1 ¹/₂" squares of red tissue paper. Each day of December, wad up a square of tissue paper and glue it to the cardboard wreath.
7. Let the wreath be a daily reminder that Christmas is a time to get ready for Jesus.

Other Ideas:
1. Paint a flat piece of cardboard and stick round, red stickers to it for each day of Advent.
2. Place a flat, paper wreath with stand-up paper candles glued on it as a centerpiece during Advent.

Wreath Patterns

Get Ready for Jesus

26

SS3812

Celebrate His Birth

Cup Centerpiece

Bible Story:
 The Christmas story. Luke 2:1-20; Matthew 2:1-20

Materials:
 Cardboard
 Pencil
 Glue
 Pointed scissors
 Tempera paint
 Paintbrush
 Glitter
 Plastic straws
 Red plastic tape
 Styrofoam™ cup
 Plastic-based clay
 Evergreen sprig
 Ribbon bow

Directions:
1. Duplicate Christmas patterns found on the following page. Cut out patterns you want to use for your Christmas arrangement.
2. Trace patterns on cardboard and cut out.
3. Paint one side of cardboard with tempera paint. Sprinkle on glitter while paint is wet. Let dry; then paint other side.
4. Put stripes on Styrofoam™ cup with red plastic tape. Glue on bow.
5. Glue (or tape) a straw to the back of each cardboard figure.
6. Place a ball of plastic-based clay in the bottom of the cup and stick the straw in it. Add the evergreen sprig.
7. Put the arrangement in your home as a reminder to celebrate Jesus' birth, the real reason for the Christmas season.

Other Ideas:
1. Outline and cut out shapes from Christmas cookie cutters.
2. Cut shapes out of Christmas cards and glue on.
3. Make cup centerpieces to represent different parts of the Christmas story.
4. Omit straw. Hang symbol with yarn for a tree ornament.

SS3812

"Celebrate His Birth" Patterns

Manger

Angel

Shepherd

Crown for Wise Man

Camel

Joseph

Mary

Stable

SS3812

Christ the Savior Is Born

Nativity Scene

Bible Story:
The Christmas story. Luke 2:1-20; Matthew 2:1-20

Materials:
Cardboard
Glue
Markers or crayons
Scissors
Clear adhesive plastic (optional)

Directions:

Stable

1. Duplicate, color, and cut out stable patterns found on pages 30-31.
2. Glue patterns on cardboard and cut out.
3. Cut along broken lines on stable. Insert pieces into slits on stable as indicated in diagram (page 31). Fold tabs and glue in place.
4. Fold and stand up stable. Add Christmas figures to it.

Figures

1. Duplicate patterns on pages 32-34.
2. Color and cut out patterns you wish to use. Glue to cardboard and cut out.
3. Slightly fold cardboard figures down the center and stand them up.
4. Let your nativity scene be a reminder of the events that took place when Christ our Savior was born.

Nativity Scene
Pattern

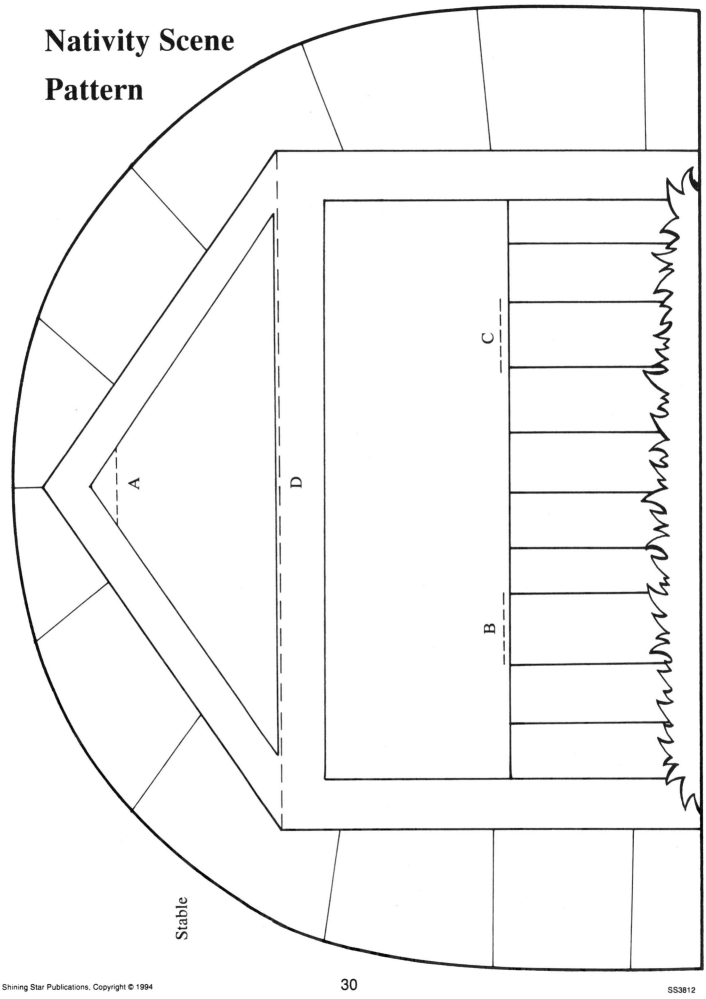

A

B

C

D

Stable

Nativity Scene Patterns

Stable top

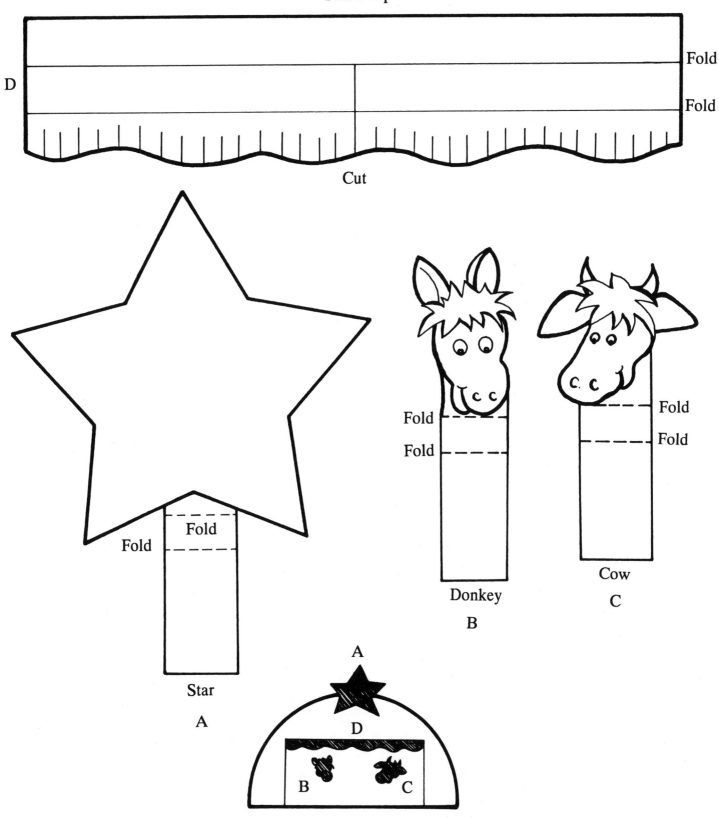

D

Fold

Fold

Cut

Fold

Fold

Fold

Star

A

Fold

Fold

Donkey

B

Fold

Fold

Cow

C

A

D

B

C

Shining Star Publications, Copyright © 1994

SS3812

Nativity Scene Patterns

Joseph

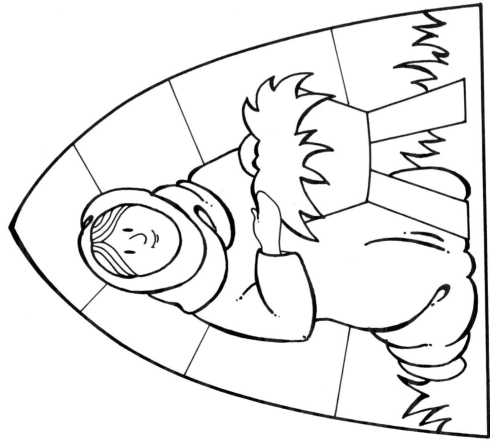

Mary and Jesus

SS3812

Nativity Scene Patterns

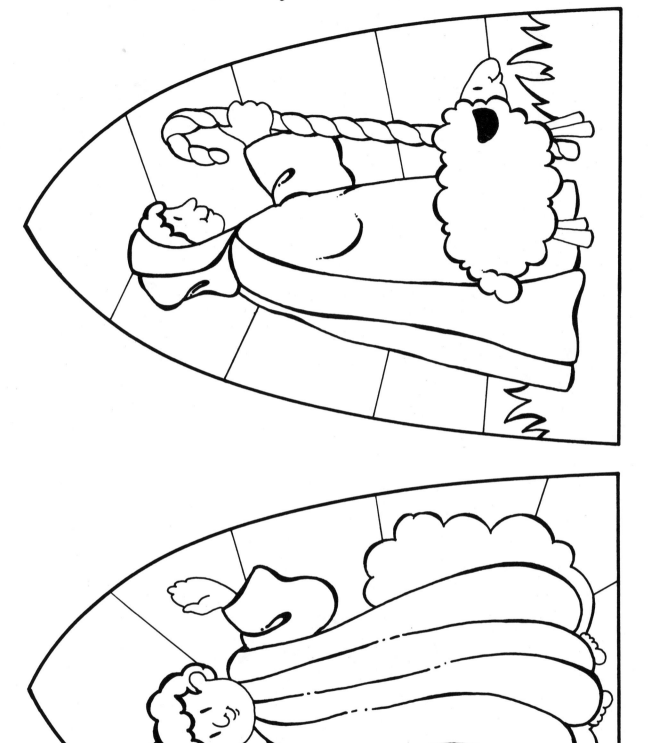

Shepherd

Angel

Shining Star Publications, Copyright © 1994

SS3812

Nativity Scene Patterns

Camel

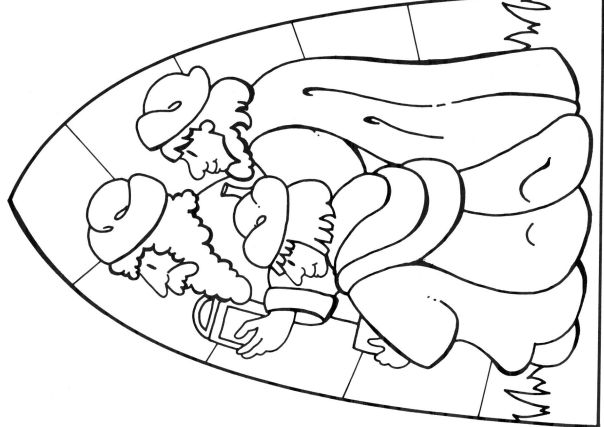

Wise Men

SS3812

We Have Seen His Star

Tree Ornament

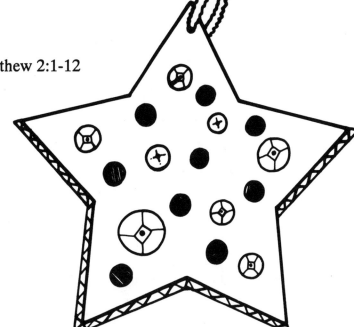

Bible Story:
>   The coming of the wise men. Matthew 2:1-12

Materials:
>   Cardboard
>   Aluminum foil
>   Colored tissue paper
>   Hole punch
>   Sequins
>   Glue
>   Pipe cleaner
>   Scissors
>   Pencil

Directions:
  1. Duplicate and cut out the star pattern on the following page.
  2. Trace the star on cardboard.
  3. Using the star pattern, trace and cut out two stars from aluminum foil and two stars from tissue paper.
  4. Use a hole punch to punch holes in the tissue paper.
  5. Glue the aluminum foil to both sides of the cardboard star.
  6. Glue the tissue paper to each piece of aluminum foil.
  7. Have an adult use pointed scissors to punch a hole through the cardboard star.
  8. Poke the pipe cleaner through the hole and loop it together.
  9. Glue on sequins, as desired.
  10. Fasten the star to the top of a Christmas tree, or hang it from a branch to remind you of the great light in the sky that led the wise men to Jesus.

Other Ideas:
  1. Hang the large star from a coat hanger. Add several smaller stars for a mobile of the stars in the Christmas sky.
  2. Add a sun and moon for a mobile of God's creation of the lights in the sky.

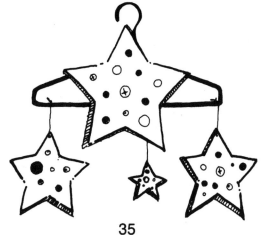

SS3812

Star Pattern

SS3812

A Dove Came Down

Mobile

Bible Story:
Jesus is baptized. Luke 3:21-22

Materials:
White tagboard or poster board
Pencil
Scissors
Marker
Yarn
Glue
Hole punch
Stapler
White feathers (optional)

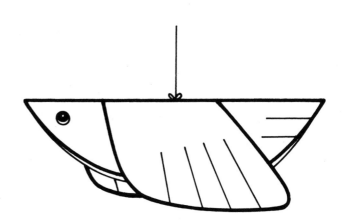

Directions: (Adult help may be needed.)
1. Duplicate and cut out dove patterns on pages 38-39.
2. Trace dove patterns on white poster board and cut them out. Cut slits in wings and body of dove.
3. Use marker to draw an eye on each side of the dove.
4. Fold dove body and staple it together as indicated.
5. Glue wings along top fold of dove's body.
6. Punch small hole at top of dove and tie a piece of yarn through it for hanging.
7. Glue some white feathers on the dove (optional).
8. Talk about how the Holy Spirit appeared as a dove when Jesus was baptized.

Other Ideas:
1. Use to tell the story of the dove sent out by Noah after the Flood.
2. Adapt bird shape for use with Creation, Elijah and the ravens, or God's care for the flowers as mentioned in the Sermon on the Mount.

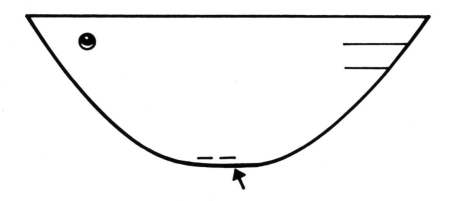

Dove Pattern

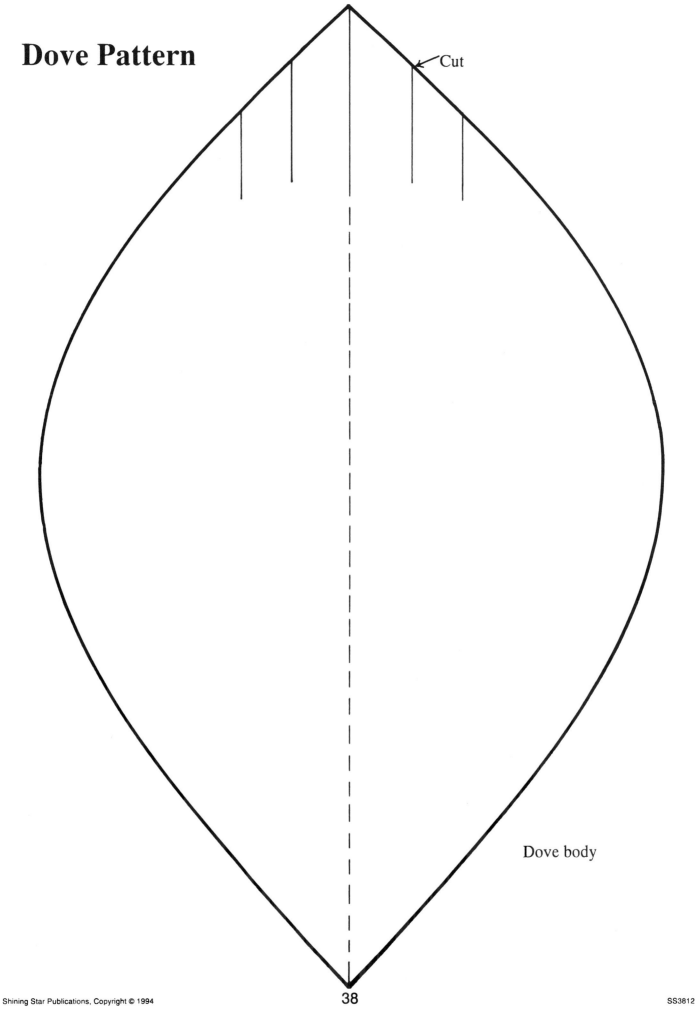

Cut

Dove body

SS3812

Dove Pattern

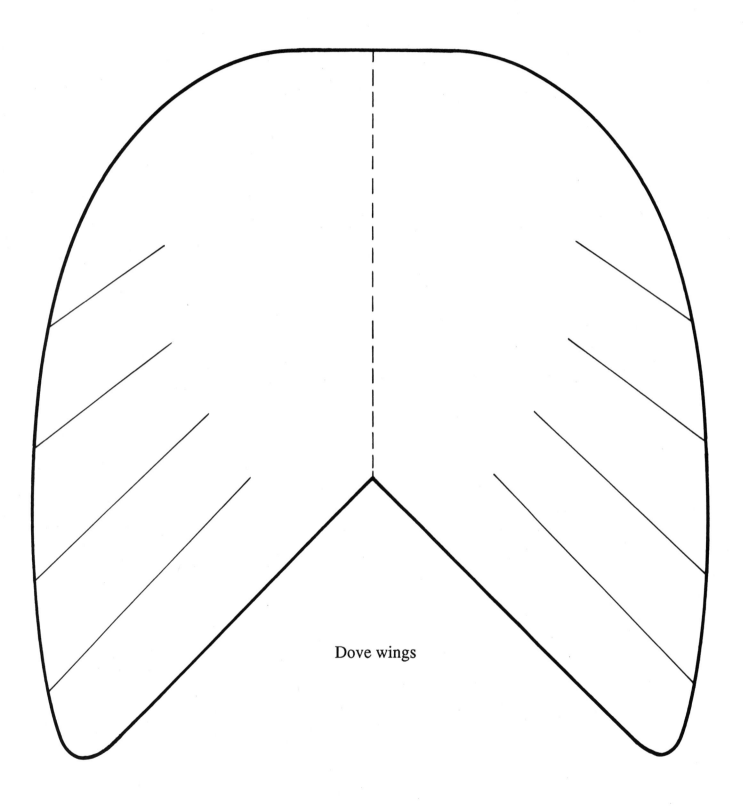

Dove wings

We Follow Jesus

Classroom Mobile

Bible Story:
Jesus chooses disciples. Matthew 4:18-22

Materials:
Cardboard
Paint
Paintbrush
Markers
Scissors
Pencil
Yarn
Hole punch

Directions: (Adult help may be needed.)
1. Outline and cut out footprint of each child.
2. Let children paint shoes on their cardboard footprints.
3. Punch hole in top of each footprint.
4. Write "We Follow Jesus" on a piece of cardboard (about 12" x 6"). Punch hole at top of cardboard strip as illustrated. Tie a loop of yarn through it for hanging mobile.
5. Punch several holes (depending on the size of your class) across bottom of cardboard strip. Tie a long piece of yarn to each hole. Thread yarn pieces through holes at tops of footprints, tying yarn in place as you do so.
6. Let the mobile serve as a reminder that you have been called to follow the Lord.

Other Ideas:
1. Make individual footprints that say, "(Name of student) Follows Jesus."
2. Color cardboard feet with markers.

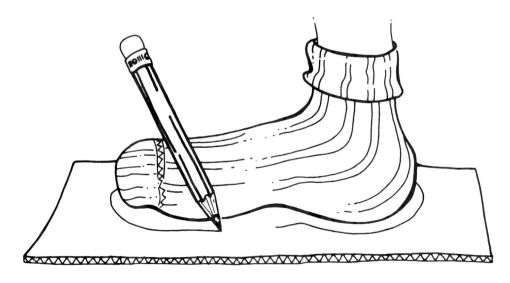

Through the Roof

Storytelling House

Bible Story:
Jesus heals a paralytic. Mark 2:1-12

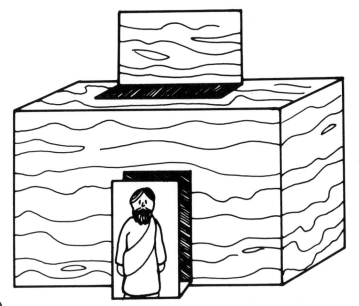

Materials:
Corrugated cardboard
Glue
Scissors
Pencil
Fine-tipped markers
Cardboard square (9" x 9")
Green and brown construction paper
Glue
Masking tape

Directions: (Adult help may be needed.)
1. Duplicate patterns on the following page. Trace and cut house pattern from corrugated cardboard. Cut out door and opening flap on top. Fold flap so it opens and closes.
2. Tear small pieces of construction paper for ground and grass. Glue over cardboard square.
3. Glue house to cardboard square base. (Reinforce sides of the house with masking tape.)
4. Use markers to color figures and cut out.
5. Fold figures so they stand.
6. Use house and stand-up figures to act out story of Jesus healing the paralyzed man.

Other Ideas:
1. Use overhead projector to enlarge patterns. Make figures from clothespins to go with larger house.
2. Have children draw their own stand-up figures for Jesus, the paralyzed man, his friends, and others at the house.
3. Paint cardboard base with tempera paint.
4. Make several houses on a cardboard base for a Palestinian village.
5. Cut house pattern from plain cardboard.

Storytelling House Patterns

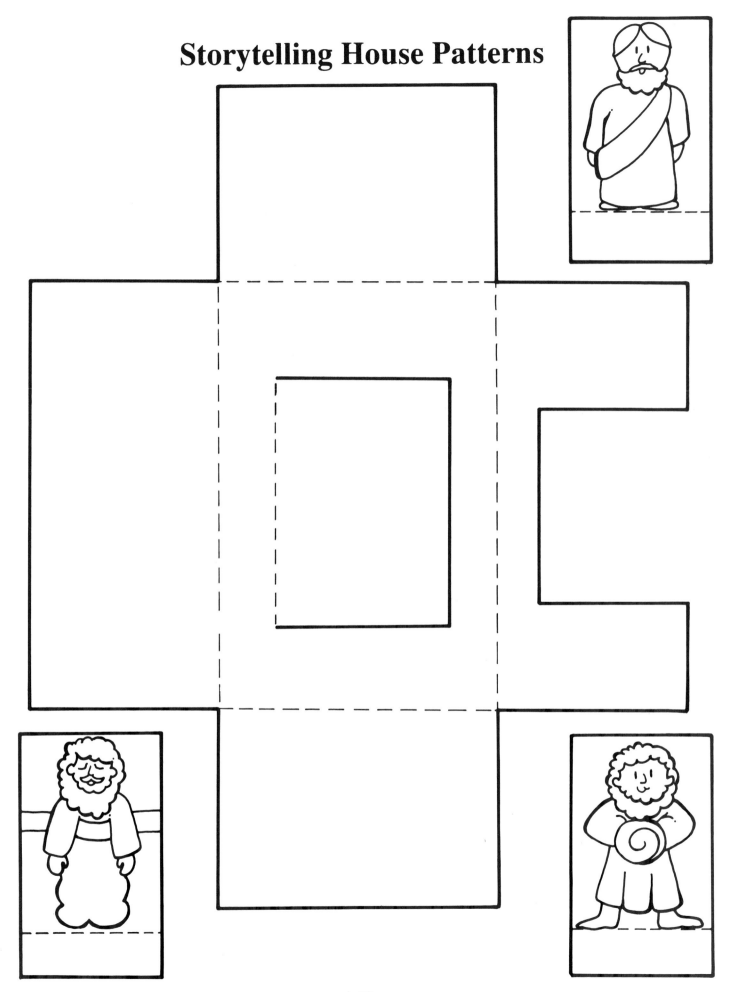

SS3812

Jesus Loves Me

Silhouette Mobile

Bible Story:
  Jesus and the children. Matthew 19:13-15

Materials:
  Cardboard
  Red and white construction paper
  White paper doilies
  Scissors
  Pencil
  Masking tape
  Yarn
  Marker
  Glue
  Overhead projector
  White paper

Directions:
1. Duplicate the heart pattern found on the following page. To make a full-sized heart, place the pattern on a fold of paper, trace, and cut out. Use the full-sized pattern to cut out a cardboard heart.
2. Tape a piece of white paper to wall. Position a child between overhead projector and paper so the child's shadow falls on the paper. Outline silhouette and cut it out.
3. Cover both sides of heart with red construction paper.
4. Cover both sides of silhouette with white construction paper.
5. Glue pieces of paper doilies on heart (leave area for message).
6. Write words "Jesus Loves (name of child)" on heart.
7. Have an adult use sharp scissors to punch a hole at the top of the silhouette and at the top of the heart, one hole a couple of inches below the other.
8. Use a piece of yarn to tie the silhouette to the bottom hole. Use a second piece of yarn to tie up the heart so it hangs like a mobile. Let your silhouette mobile remind you that Jesus loves you.

Other Ideas:
1. Use black, tan, or pink paper for the silhouette.
2. Add stickers, sequins, pieces of bright ribbon, or other decorative scraps to the heart.
3. Use yarn and/or markers to add hair and other features to silhouette.
4. Paint the heart and silhouette with tempera paint.

Heart Pattern

Cut

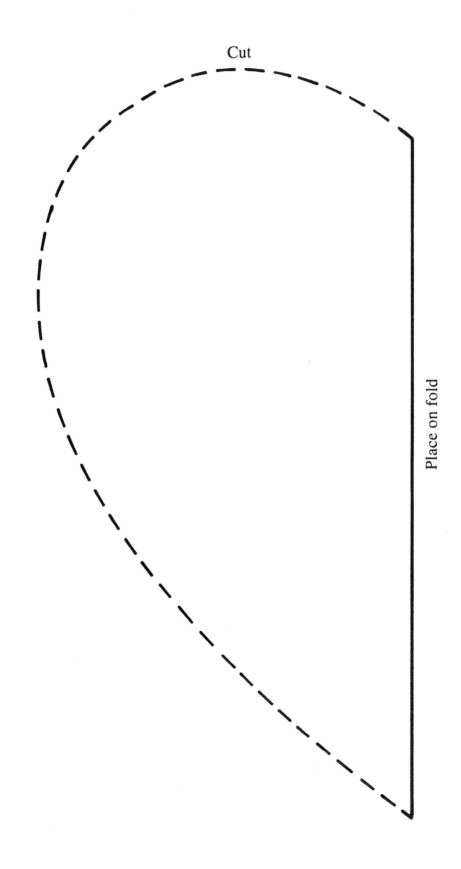

Place on fold

SS3812

God's Love Is Forever

Shadow Puppets

Bible Story:
The prodigal son. Luke 15:11-32

Materials:
Cardboard
Pencil
Scissors
Wire coat hangers
Masking tape
Desk lamp
Ruler
Sheer cloth
Two cardboard rolls

Directions:
Shadow Screen
1. Make a screen by cutting a square or rectangle of cardboard the size you want to use. Measure and cut out the inside section of the cardboard about 2" from all sides for a frame.
2. Cut a piece of sheer cloth about 1¹/₂" longer on all sides than the cardboard frame. Fold the cloth over the frame and tape it in place.
3. Glue a cardboard roll to the bottom of each side of the frame. Stand it upright on the edge of a table or chair with the desk lamp behind it.

Puppets
1. Duplicate and cut out the patterns found on the following page.
2. Trace the patterns on cardboard and cut them out. Tape pieces of wire clothes hangers to the figures for handles.
3. Hold the puppets between the screen and light moving them to act out the story.

Other Ideas:
1. Make shadow puppets to act out other Bible stories.
2. Have the children draw figures to cut out and use in telling Bible stories or cut figures from catalogs or magazines.

                                                                                          SS3812

Shadow Puppet Patterns

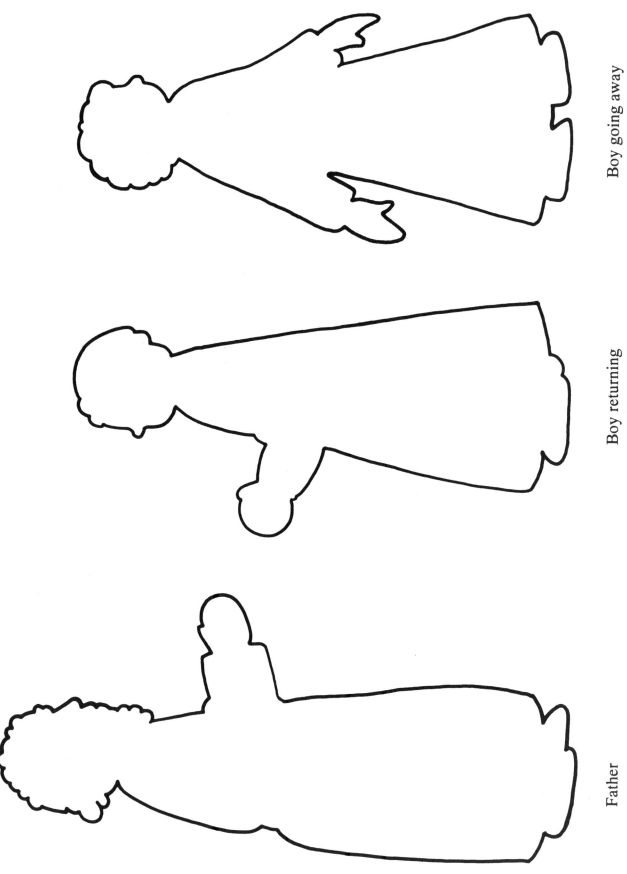

Boy going away

Boy returning

Father

Shining Star Publications, Copyright © 1994

SS3812

Jesus Helps People

Stick Puppets

Bible Story:
Stories of Jesus' miracles. The Four Gospels

Materials:
Cardboard
Pencil
Glue
Scissors
Markers or crayons
Craft sticks
Two cardboard tubes
Clear adhesive plastic (optional)

Directions: (Adult help may be needed.)

Tabletop Puppet Theater

1. Duplicate and cut out the theater pattern found on page 48. Glue the theater to cardboard and cut it out.
2. Use markers to decorate the theater. For more permanency, cover with clear adhesive plastic.
3. Glue an upright cardboard roll to each side of the theater on the back to make it stand up.
4. Stand the theater at the edge of a table. Use puppets behind it to tell stories of Jesus and His love for other people.

Puppets

1. Choose puppet patterns on pages 49-50 to illustrate the Bible story you wish to teach. Duplicate and cut out the patterns.
2. Glue patterns to cardboard and cut out.
3. Use markers to decorate each puppet. Cover them with clear adhesive plastic for more permanency.
4. Glue craft sticks to the back of the puppets for handles.

Other Ideas:

1. Use tempera to paint puppets and theater.
2. Make a variety of puppets to keep on hand in the classroom for use with Bible stories throughout the year.
3. Encourage children to write scripts for puppet presentations.

Bibleland Theater

48

SS3812

"Jesus Helps People" Patterns

Jesus

"Jesus Helps People" Patterns

SS3812

Sing Hosanna

Palm Sunday Palm Branch

Bible Story:
Jesus rides into Jerusalem. Mark 11:1-10

Materials:
Corrugated cardboard
Pencil
Scissors
Green tempera paint
Paintbrush
Markers or crayons
Glue

Directions: (Adult help may be needed.)
1. Duplicate pattern found on following page.
2. Trace palm shape on corrugated cardboard with lines going in a horizontal direction to the sides of the branch, as illustrated above.
3. Paint one side of the cardboard branch green.
4. Fringe the sides of the branch by cutting triangular slits along the cardboard ridges (optional).
5. Cut and color "Sing Hosanna" strip. Glue it to the center of the palm branch.
6. Put up your completed palm branch as a reminder of the triumphant entry when children waved palm branches and sang "Hosanna" to Jesus, their King.

Other Ideas:
1. Let children do their own lettering for the "Sing Hosanna" strip.
2. Write the words to a Palm Sunday song in the center of the palm branch.
3. Cut the branch out of plain cardboard; then color it with crayon or paint.
4. Use the branches for a class Palm Sunday procession.
5. Mount branches on Palm Sunday bulletin board.

Palm Branch Patterns

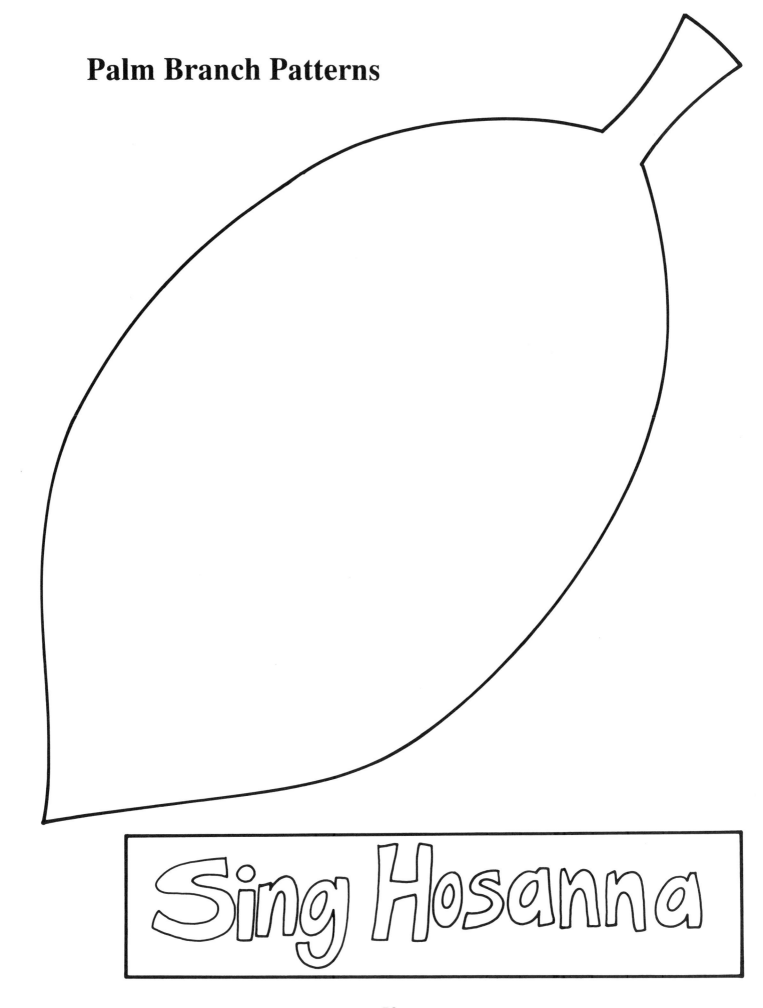

Sing Hosanna

SS3812

He Is Risen

Pressed-Leaf Collage

Bible Story:
Jesus is alive. Luke 24:1-12

Materials:
Cardboard (9 ½" x 11")
Blue tempera paint
Paintbrush
Corrugated cardboard
Burlap
Leaves
Newspaper
Heavy book
Glue
Masking tape
Markers
Paper clip
Scissors
Pencil

Directions: (Adult help may be needed.)
1. Press leaves by placing them between several layers of newspapers and setting them under a heavy book for several days.
2. Duplicate and cut out patterns on the following page.
3. Cut a piece of burlap large enough to cover the bottom three-fourths of the 9 ½" x 11" piece of cardboard. Glue on burlap.
4. To represent the sky, paint the cardboard blue in the area above the burlap. Let dry.
5. Trace and cut out tomb and stone patterns from corrugated cardboard.
6. Glue tomb to burlap. Glue stone beside open door with lines on cardboard going opposite direction from tomb.
7. Glue pressed leaves around the tomb.
8. Use markers to decorate the open tomb entrance pattern. Glue it on the tomb.
9. Tape a paper clip to the back of picture for hanging.
10. Let your picture remind you of the angel's message "Jesus Is Alive!"

Other Ideas:
1. Glue squares of colored tissue paper around open tomb.
2. Draw an angel inside the tomb.
3. Add pressed flowers to picture.

"He Is Risen" Patterns

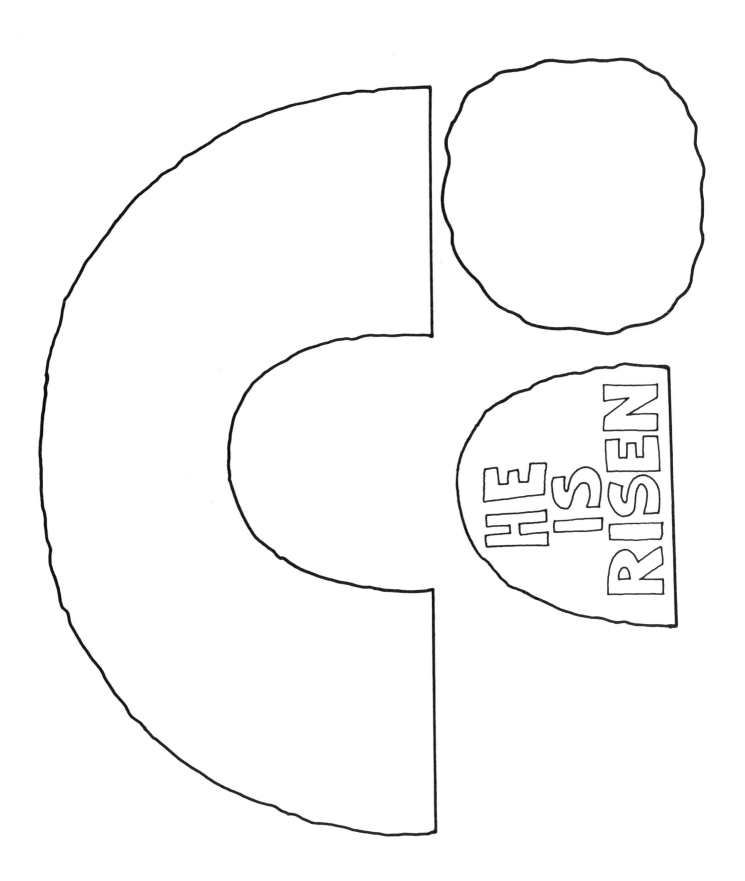

SS3812

The Holy Spirit Comes

Rice Plaque

Bible Story:
Pentecost. Acts 2:1-4

Materials:
Cardboard
Rice
Red food coloring
Bowl
Glue
Tray
Yarn
Scissors
Pencil

Directions: (Adult help may be needed.)
1. Duplicate the dove pattern on the following page.
2. Cut out the circle and trace it on a piece of cardboard. Cut out the cardboard circle.
3. Cut out the dove shape and trace it on the cardboard circle.
4. Punch a hole at the top of the cardboard and tie a loop of yarn through for a hanger.
5. Dye rice in a bowl with a mixture of red food coloring and water. Spread rice on a tray to dry.
6. Spread glue on dove shape and sprinkle with white rice.
7. Spread glue around dove shape on cardboard circle and sprinkle with red rice.
8. Talk about how the Holy Spirit, who appeared as a dove at Jesus' baptism and came to Jesus' followers at Pentecost.

Other Ideas:
1. Dye background rice blue to use plaque with a lesson on Jesus' baptism.
2. Enlarge dove shape and put on a round pizza cardboard.

SS3812

"The Holy Spirit Comes" Pattern

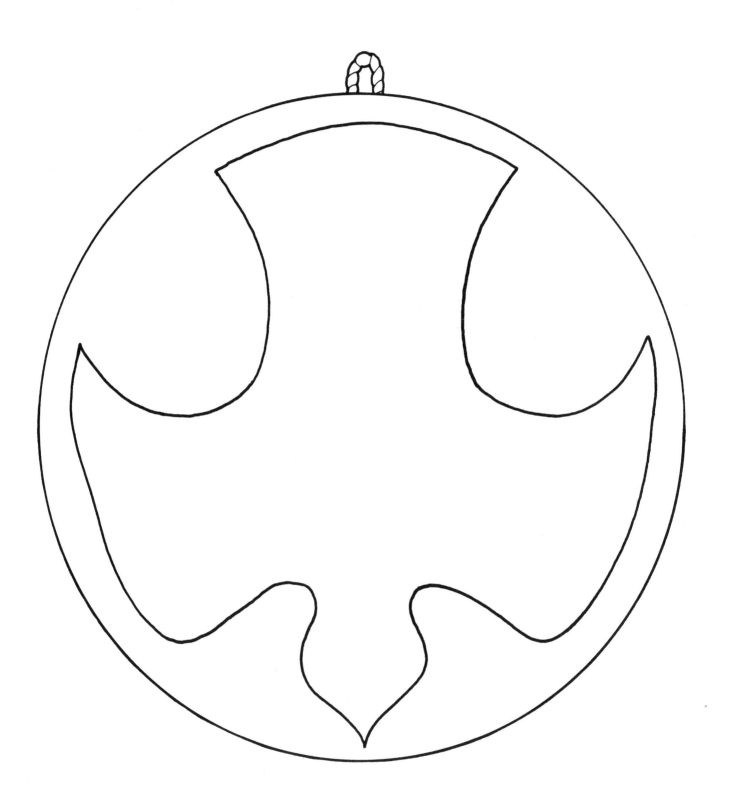

SS3812

Witness for the Lord

Aluminum Foil Plaque

Bible Story:
How early Christians lived. Acts 2:42-47

Materials:
Corrugated cardboard
Plain cardboard
Pencil
Scissors
Heavy aluminum foil
Black shoe polish
Cloth
Clear acrylic sealer
Paintbrush
Glue
Wooden spoon (optional)
Paper clip
Tape

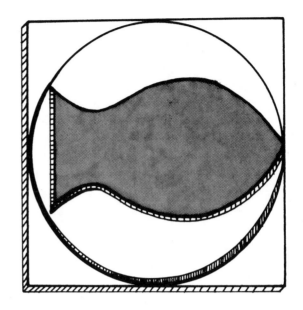

Directions:
1. Duplicate and cut out patterns on the following page.
2. Trace and cut square and fish shapes from plain cardboard.
3. Trace and cut circle from corrugated cardboard.
4. Glue circle in middle of square; then glue fish to middle of circle.
5. Cut a square of aluminum foil, 1" longer on each side than cardboard square. Place foil loosely over entire fish plaque and fold foil around the back.
6. Being very careful not to tear foil, smooth it down around design on plaque. If you wish, use the back of a wooden spoon to work foil over outlines and ridges of pattern. Glue foil on back of plaque when finished.
7. Rub black shoe polish over foil; then wipe off for an "antique" effect. Brush with clear acrylic sealer when finished.
8. Tape a paper clip to back of plaque for hanging.
9. The fish was used as a symbol for Christianity in New Testament days. Let your fish plaque serve as a reminder to live life as a faithful witness, as the early Christians did.

Other Ideas:
1. Make a creation plaque by placing a leaf or other "found" nature item in the center of the plaque.
2. Make the plaque with a different Christian symbol cut out of cardboard.

SS3812

"Witness for the Lord" Patterns

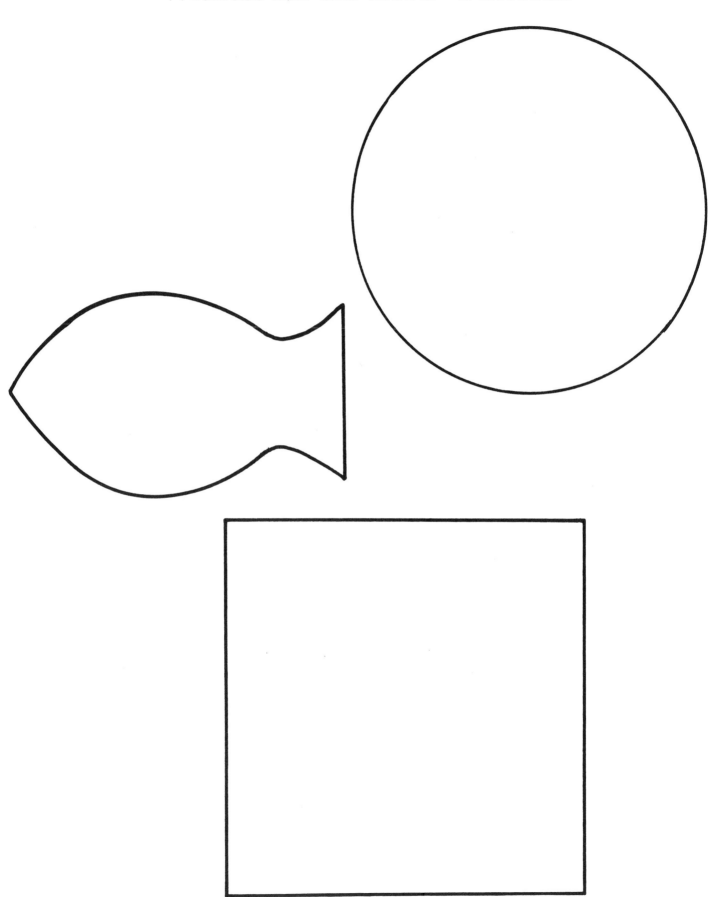

SS3812

Spread the Good Word

Boat

Bible Story:
God calls Paul and Barnabas to spread His Word. Acts 13:2-3

Materials:
Corrugated cardboard
Tempera paint (optional)
Paintbrush
Two 8" drinking straws
Scissors
Glue
Pencil
Stapler
Oil-based clay
Markers or crayons

Directions:
1. Duplicate and cut out patterns on pages 60-61.
2. Trace boat and sail shapes on corrugated cardboard and cut them out.
3. Fold up two sides of boat and staple ends together.
4. Paint boat and sail with tempera paint (optional). Let dry.
5. Use markers to decorate "Spread the Good Word" pattern pieces. Glue words on sail.
6. Staple two straws together to make a capital "T."
7. Fold top of sail over top straw and staple in place. Glue sail along vertical straw.
8. Stick end of straw in a ball of oil-based clay and set it in the middle of the boat.
9. Look through Acts 13-28 to find references to some of the places Paul went to spread God's Word. Talk about ways missionaries travel today to spread God's Word.

Other Ideas:
1. Use colored poster board for boat and sail. Add lettering and boat details with markers.
2. Accordion fold a piece of construction paper for sail or use it straight.

Boat Pattern

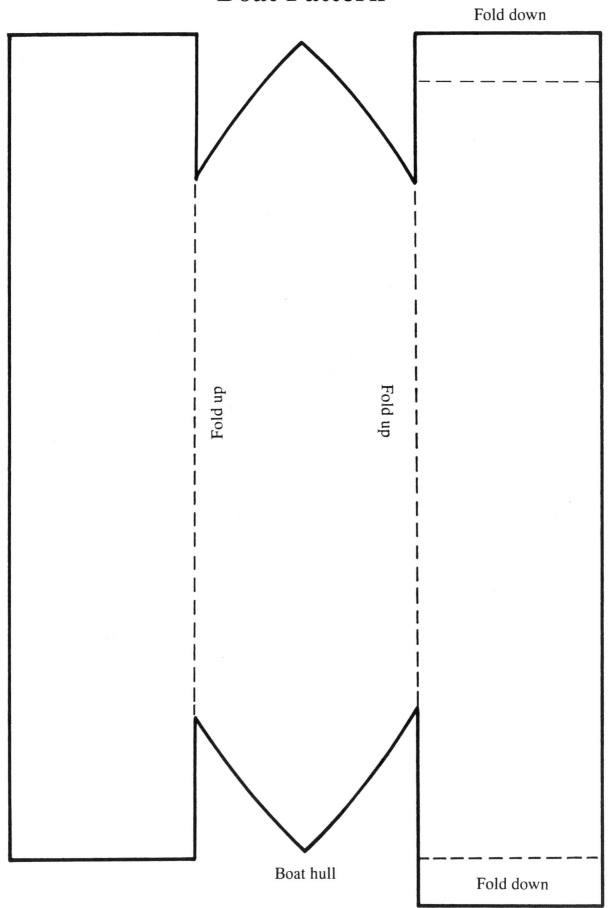

Fold down

Fold up

Fold up

Boat hull

Fold down

SS3812

Boat Patterns

Boat sail

Believe in Jesus

Cross Plaque

Bible Story:
Paul and the Philippian jailer. Acts 16:16-34

Materials:
Poster board
Colored glue
Scissors
Eight craft sticks (4 1/2" long)
Yarn
Glue

Directions:
1. Cut 4 1/4" x 4 1/4" square of poster board.
2. Glue first four craft sticks around square as indicated in diagram. Back with last four sticks.
3. Use colored glue to draw a cross in the square. Use lines or dots to draw in cross shape. Use colored glue to also decorate craft sticks, if you wish.
4. Cut an 8" piece of yarn. Tie to each side of top for a hanger.
5. Let your cross picture serve as a reminder of Paul's words in Acts 16:31 to the jailer at Philippi, "Believe in the Lord Jesus, and you will be saved."

Other Ideas:
1. Use markers to draw pictures inside frame.
2. Make cross out of pieces of yarn.
3. Glue pictures from old Christmas cards inside frame.

Jumping for Joy

String Puppet

Bible Story:
Peter and John heal a lame man. Acts 3:1-9

Materials:
Poster board
Markers or crayons
Pencil
Scissors
Glue
String
Craft stick
Two washers

Directions:
1. Duplicate and cut out patterns found on following page. Trace and cut shapes from poster board.
2. Use markers to color man's face and clothes.
3. Arrange pieces in order, facedown. Attach strings with glue as indicated in diagram.
4. Glue washer to back of each foot.
5. Tie top string to center of craft stick. Cut strings to go from ends of craft stick to hands. Tie one end of each string to craft stick; glue other end to a puppet hand.
6. Tell story of Peter and John healing a crippled man. Move craft stick to make puppet jump for joy when he is healed.

Other Ideas:
1. Color patterns and glue them to cardboard pieces.
2. Cover puppet with cloth or construction paper.
3. Sing song "Silver and Gold Have I None" moving puppet at appropriate lines.

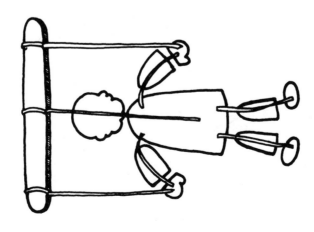

String Puppet Patterns

SS3812